After All

at the University of Florida

After All

Poems

Robert B. Cumming

Iris Press Chapbook Series
Oak Ridge, Tennessee

Copyright © 2022 by Robert B. Cumming

All rights reserved. No portion of this book may be reproduced in any form or by any means, including electronic storage and retrieval systems, without explicit, prior written permission of the author, except for brief passages excerpted for review and critical purposes.

ISBN: 978-1-60454-513-5

"Each Rainbow" first appeared in the *Asheville Poetry Review* (spring/summer 1996)

cover photo by Wallace Chester Cumming

book and cover design by Robert B. Cumming, Jr.

Iris Publishing Group, Inc.
www.irisbooks.com

Contents

Publisher's Note • 9

•

Ephemera • 13
Once We Were Four • 15
The Mechanics of Loss • 16
A Small Map of Forever • 17
The Tyranny of *Now* • 19
Favorite Season • 21
She Dreams • 22
An Inadvertent Glance • 23
Adrift • 24
To Carmen in May • 25
Three Years After • 26
The River • 27
After All • 29
My Mind Is a Beehive • 30
Frugality • 31
Convenience • 32
Each Rainbow • 33
Long-Distance Runner • 34

•

Bob Cumming Tributes • 37
About Bob Cumming • 43

for Carmen Montes Cumming

May 9, 1931-May 27, 2015

Publisher's Note

After Lana Austin emailed me that a group of authors and friends of Iris Press created a GoFundMe fundraiser to show appreciation and support for the press, my first thought was, "Wait…. What?"

When I visited the website, it had already reached its goal of $2000+. The GoFundMe description suggested that Iris Press could use some of the money to publish a book by my father and me. I had self-published my chapbook, *Green Lion*, in 2019. I have been urging my father to publish a collection of his poems. I appreciate the GoFundMe contributors for giving me an extra boost of motivation to publish it.

After my father bought Iris Press twenty-five years ago, he also started writing poetry in fixed forms. The challenge of composing fixed poetic forms is following the rules, breaking them when needed, and making the language and syntax sound natural. He improved his poetry by reading many poetry books and journals.

My father has an extensive poetry collection that he bought over the years. Many of the books were signed by the authors at readings or events. He also studied the craft of poetry. For example, several years ago, he bought *A Little Book on Form: An Exploration into the Formal Imagination of Poetry* by Robert Hass. For almost a decade, he regularly attended a monthly poetry group with five or six people who offered suggestions about revising each other's poems.

For many years, my father has been working on revising his poetry for a collection. He had created a list of his poems that were finished or nearly finished. I used that list to put his poems into a manuscript. I want to thank Lana Austin, KB Ballentine, Thomas Alan Holmes, and Linda Parsons for their help editing the manuscript. Although his work didn't need much revision, their suggestions and encouragement were very helpful.

As I was reading the manuscript, I started crying. I had already read different versions of these poems over the years, but their combined impact greatly affected me with his ruminations about aging, mortality, and loss. The three poems he wrote about my mother were a gut punch. My father will be ninety-four in October 2022, and he has been facing health challenges.

I also shed happy tears because I knew I could publish this exceptional—in my biased opinion—book. I am grateful for our Iris Press family who donated money as a gesture of support for our work over the years.

After my father silently read the manuscript, I asked what he thought about it. He said, "Those poems are pretty good." I said, "Yes. Yes, they are *really* good."

—Beto Cumming
September 2022

Ephemera

for Juan Antonio Corretjer

The blush of spring, the ever-changing dance—
but nothing lasts forever, or for long—
there's beauty in all verses of the song.
How quick it disappears, a blink! a glance!

How vivid every passing moment seems
as if life's frightful magic were alive
and struggling through the darkness to revive
the insubstantial currency of dreams.
The epic we conjecture always gleams.
Longevity depends on circumstance,
but soon we're gone without a trace or chance.
No use in adding up the cost
and calculating what is lost—
the blush of spring, the ever-changing dance—

The sky! The sky! The endless stream of wings
to fade away like angels in the snow
and fall, alas, proud Passenger, and go
to lands of ether where the dodo sings.
Oblivion! The Valley of the Kings:
Pretentious monuments soon move along,
though built to be eternal, stout and strong,
they disappear as all things must,
collapsing slowly into dust,
but nothing lasts forever, or for long—

A symphony! A symphony unbound,
the rhythm makes the human soul complete:
persistence of the stout and rhythmic beat,
the unexpected burst of joyous sound.
The music does consistently astound
and raise the spirits of the lively throng,
but joy in living also must belong
to moments when the churchbells ring,
when mountains and the meadows sing.
There's beauty in all verses of the song.

A flash of lightning gilds the midnight sky,
illuminates an instant in the dark
and then is gone without another spark,
without a signpost to remember by.
And fighting through the twilight to defy
the ever-moving clock in its advance,
the hopeless urge to blunt time's fearsome lance.
A life moves on; the die is cast
with neither future nor a past.
How quick it disappears, a blink! a glance!

Once We Were Four

Remembering Dave
October 31, 1929-May 11, 2013

Once we were four and young,
believing we were invincible
on that dark, unsteady ground.
My brothers also

believed we were invincible,
equal to any challenge.
My brothers also,
close in age and outlook,

equal to any challenge
in this hostile and uncertain world.
Close in age and outlook,
with time the great equalizer

in this hostile and uncertain world,
we knew we were lucky.
With time the great equalizer
nothing was impossible.

We knew we were lucky:
amazing parents for whom
nothing was impossible
with hard work and study.

Amazing parents for whom
I, the least of this band of brothers
with hard work and study
the last one standing—

I, the least of this band of brothers.
Once we were four, and I,
the last one standing
on this dark, unsteady ground.

The Mechanics of Loss

This shall too soon completely disappear,
this vivid world of sights & sounds & smells,
without a trace to show that we were here.

Some days are lower key, and almost drear,
a softer scene all painted in pastels.
This too shall soon completely disappear.

Those dearest of companions year to year,
those sad departures made without farewells,
and not a trace to show that we were here.

The stories we invent in hope or fear,
the fabric of a life, the jokes, the spells,
these too shall soon completely disappear

along with all the gadgets we hold dear,
and gone, the compromise each day compels
without a trace to show that we were here,

the details of a life that we revere,
the cave in which the human spirit dwells:
These all shall soon completely disappear
without a trace to show that we were here.

A Small Map of Forever

for Adelaide Crapsey

Till I come on the Word in this good Book, I used to think a mountain was the standingest object in the sight o' God. Hit says here they go skipping and hopping like sheep, a-rising and a-falling. These hills are jist dirt waves, washing through eternity. My brethren, they hain't a valley so low but what hit'll rise again. They hain't a hill standing so proud but hit'll sink to the low ground o' sorrow.

—from Brother Sim Mobberly's sermon
in James Still's *River of Earth*

Listen!
All things you see
are finite, those you hear
will fade like morning mist and soon
be gone.

And though
we live our days
in stark relentless search
for meaning here on tiny Earth,
we hold

to myths
of ages past
with spirits floating through
a homocentric universe—
live ghosts

and shades
whose dark shadows
color all of our lives.
Your ripple in the sea of time
is small

but still
persists until
it reaches distant shores.
Our vision always works within
a space

set by
human scale and
prolonged experience.
And as in all things human, soon
it will

be gone.
The joy of life
lies not with permanence,
but how we live with what we know.
Listen!

The Tyranny of *Now*

for Daniel Corrie

Though lost
in shallow seas
of time's relentless thrust,
and *past* is only memory,
fiction,

a sharp
and vivid dream,
imagined victories
and defeats. The *future* also
dreamlike,

just a
phantom guess, while
each *now*: a strobe of light
in fields of shadow, fading fast
and gone.

And out
among the stars
where *past* and *future* blend,
now still lives its nonexistent
life and

carries
on its narrow
shoulders all the weight of
what is real in the universe,
what lasts,

and this
kaleidoscope,
the tyranny of *now*,
is all we have to anchor to
this earth,

fiction,
a shaky ground,
but one thing feels true: We
still, through successive *nows* move on,
though lost.

Favorite Season

Fall is her favorite season. I can tell
because of how she frolics through the leaves.
The limpid air bites back, as twilight weaves
a crazy quilt of color, sound and smell.
She dances through the dusk and doesn't dwell
on winter's coming darkness, never grieves
for summer's fading memory. She believes
that life is in the instant, living well.

But I am more reflective, and ahead
I see dark clouds, the loss of friends, and pain;
though still, regarded from a broader view,
the magic of each day unfolds instead,
now more intense, a song of loss and gain.
I think that fall's my favorite season too.

She Dreams

A muffled growl, a soft staccato bark—
a fitful forefoot paws the languid air.
"She dreams," I think. "She penetrates the dark
recesses of some murky stygian lair."
I also dream, but not of cats who dare
to infiltrate my designated space.
I dream of rugged autumn trails where
we struggle through the tangled forest lace.
She moves with such intensity and grace,
a proper part of nature so it seems,
that I expect, and see, a focused face
of ardent wakefulness, and yet *she dreams!*
Through wind, rain, fleas, and frequent scenes of strife,
we dreamers share a buoyant view of life.

An Inadvertent Glance

I saw my mother's hands, my father's face
while walking past a mirror on the wall.
His stern, reproving glare, her gnarled grace

are images I never will erase.
How strange! An inadvertent glance was all,
I saw my mother's hands, my father's face.

In anxious moving all around this place,
I dream them here & vividly recall
his stern, reproving glare, her gnarled grace,

their years of wisdom gone without a trace.
But through the mist I hear the dodo's call
and see my mother's hands, my father's face,

their pushing on through victories & loss
with time's relentless, stark intent to quell
his stern, reproving glare, her gnarled grace,

their lives an endless struggle everyplace,
but life is made of moments, large & small:
I saw my mother's hands, my father's face,
his stern, reproving glare, her gnarled grace.

Adrift

for Carmen, forever

Adrift! My life companion gone. That vast
uncharted country, silent, lacking speech,
where darkness dwells, where shades of night approach.
The skies above this homestead: overcast.
And moving on, resisting hell's cold grasp
of all those missing moments, each by each,
while lurking within memory's long reach—
the sparkling, fictive earthscape of the past.

But I'm perhaps most fortunate of men
because a chance encounter long ago
led to a life of wonder, which retains
its magic and its majesty, and when,
through all this ruin now, the afterglow
still burnishes the beauty that remains.

To Carmen in May

May 9, 2017

a full two years and counting
since you left and I
through all these restless sable nights
still dream you near
still feel your presence nigh
this aching absence always making clear
the sparkling sky above our early Mays
remembering the hopes we faced together
I stop and rest a while and think a prayer
it makes me more reflective now
we never lost the beauty that we gained
and through the somber clouds of late Decembers
you shaped the joys and textures of our days
this tiny house remembers us as one
and I judge every move
by how you would approve

Three Years After

This love! It doesn't stop with death, you know,
but changes colors with the passing years.
Through summer's sunshine with its golden glow
the somber blue of winter soon appears.
This love of ours still glitters through the tears,
"in health or sickness until death us part,"
but death will never quench what perseveres—
undying flame that soothes a broken heart.
This fragile planet struggles to avert
catastrophe, but with a closer lens,
through joy and pain you helped us create art
within the human song that never ends.
    The night is vast and lacking form, although
    the candle in the dark is still aglow.

The River

for Joseph Enzweiler
October 21, 1950-April 16, 2011

Incomprehensible, the flow of time
across the rugged dreamscape of the mind:
We hear the distant murmur of the wind
and the muffled music of thunder
and pause where hopes and species go to die
along the swiftly flowing river.

The ever-changing scenes along the river,
the irreversibility of time,
and watching nature's beauty slowly die,
a heavy weight of sorrow on the mind.
We sense the deep and somber voice of thunder,
the plaintive whisper of the wind.

And noticing the turbulence of wind
wrestling with the trees along the river,
and hearing through the night the roar of thunder,
we struggle with the cruelty of time,
the unpredictable, unsettled mind
that knows all living things must die.

The ancient legends never want to die,
and Zeus, with all his fury, drives the wind.
It seems that human folly's on his mind—
the planet's slow destruction kills the river.
We watch him, in his anger, throughout time,
deploy his chosen weapon: thunder.

The coming storms will shake the sky like thunder;
the sea will rise and island lands will die;
whole ecosystems will run out of time.
Our way of life will vanish in the wind
while billionaires are sleeping by the river,
where out of sight means out of mind.

The current mass extinction blasts the mind—
this fragile Earth beset with storms and thunder.
Such beauty still depending on the river,
but now condemned to prematurely die,
now slowly disappearing in the wind,
the strange perversity of time.

Though seeing meaning die, the troubled mind
survives these angry days of wind and thunder,
and time, still flowing with the river.

After All

We are now witnessing a spectacle which is truly extraordinary, unique in the history of poetry: every poet is going off by himself with his own flute, and playing the songs he pleases. For the first time since the beginning of poetry, poets have stopped singing bass.

—Mallarmé, 1891

Though, after all, we reach out, from a place
alive with birdsong, whispering of trees,
the wild, obsessive buzzing of the bees,
and all of nature's calm relentless grace,
to hold a hand, to touch a human face
and listen well for heartbeats on the breeze,
to speak with all the clarity we please
and hear the flute, the throbbing of the bass.

There's something in the spirit that denies
the stark cacophony that I recall.
Let's slow it down before the sparkle dies,
and hope, if we're attentive when we call,
the soft and rhythmic human voice replies—
the joy is in the singing, after all.

My Mind Is a Beehive

My mind is just a beehive, a place of mindless clutter, with dust of many aimless years scattered on the floor. It's like a silent movie, all emotion with no sound except the background music's constant buzz, each face contorted, eyes spread wide, each tiny heart a flutter. Each worker knows not what the work is for. My brain is withered, called upon to house a lifetime's fuzz. Each neuron serves its mindless role, oblivious of spark or goal, unaware of things that really matter. Acknowledge then the frenzy of the swarm! The vision's cold, and yet the body's warm.

Frugality

Depression's awkward child, I early learned
to clean my plate, to always scrimp and save,
and make the most of every dollar earned
in ordered, measured marching toward the grave.
Each piece of string, each random thing we'd crave,
but food came first. The enemy was waste.
We'd dream of feasts, the parties rich folks gave,
but hunger soon democratizes taste.
As times grew fat, my palate still embraced
each morsel on the plate: I'd surely try it!
And at each meal the stacks of food I faced
would blast a hole in any kind of diet.
With tattered heart, expanding waist, decay,
I learned at last to throw some things away.

Convenience

we were not made in its image
but from the beginning we believed in it
not for the pure appeasement of hunger
but for its availability and its comfort
it could command our devotion
beyond question and without our consent
and by whatever name we have called it
in its name love has been set aside
unmeasured time has been devoted to it
forests have been erased and rivers poisoned
and truth has been compromised for it
wars have been sanctified by it
we believe that we have a right to it
even though it belongs to no one
we carry a way back to it
everywhere we go
we are sure that it is saving something
we consider it our personal savior
all we have to pay for it is ourselves

Each Rainbow

Each rainbow you see is yours alone
the scientists say. No other vantage point
can catch those same raindrops bending light,
can build that same glowing image in the dusk.

The scientists say no other vantage point
aside from wavelength and quantum theory
can build that same glowing image in the dusk.
But what does science know of color

aside from wavelength and quantum theory?
Prisms bend, prisms strain the light,
but what does science know of color—
what does science know of dreams?

Prisms bend, prisms strain the light
while color does its major work inside.
What does science know of dreams
that tint the checkered landscape of our lives?

While color does its major work inside
where lurk those incandescent myths
that tint the checkered landscape of our lives,
the ghosts of rainbows past still linger here.

Where lurk those incandescent myths
raising hope for some illusive treasure?
The ghosts of rainbows past still linger, here
to feast upon and chew 'til every dream

raises hope for some illusive treasure.
Each rainbow you see is yours alone
to feast upon and chew 'til every dream
can catch those same raindrops bending light.

Long-Distance Runner

The drive to struggle toward a goal
and strain to see beyond the bend,
to move ahead, to push, to roll,

and think that youth would never end
are natural enough, although
still not enough to change, extend

or interrupt the steady flow—
at times in sweat through summer heat,
at times to slog through ice and snow,

the pace is neither slack nor fleet—
the slap, slap, slap of running shoes
consumes the dark and empty street.

The race is there to win or lose,
a random course without design,
without the means to plan or choose

the doubtful path, or redefine
the many miles I have tread,
and there, too soon, the finish line,

now clearly visible ahead
with so much story left unsaid.

Bob Cumming Tributes

Bob Cumming is a passionate editor and publisher for Iris Press. His reading, and therefore his publishing, taste is eclectic and features a variety of authors, genres, and material. Bob is a worker and is dedicated to the writers he publishes, overwhelmingly generous in sharing his knowledge and skill, and fiercely dependable in supporting his authors and friends. A talented and detailed writer in his own right, Bob's poetry is beautifully crafted and comes from his heart. His work will certainly touch the reader's heart.

—KB Ballentine

When I submitted my book, *Kaleidoscope,* for consideration by Iris Press, I just had a feeling this might be the right press for the book, and I was correct. After winning awards for publication on three chapbooks and two of my three full-length books, I always felt that I could have no better, more considerate, more kind, more solicitous editor than Bob. I remember his deep voice when we first spoke. Beto and Bob made for a great publishing experience for a writer, and they allowed me major input into my cover. I've never had such an easy time getting a book into print as I did with Bob (and Beto) and will remain forever grateful. They are true gentlemen.

—Tina Barr

Bob Cumming knows the fine juncture where intellect and exuberance meet. He has pitched a camp meeting revival tent at that intersection, and from there Iris Press works its magic. How else to explain a science PhD at the Oak Ridge National Lab who acquires Iris Press in order to publish writing he loves? Gratitude to Beto and Carmen Montes (how we miss her!), who have worked alongside Bob to bring out book after beautiful book since 1996. Wonder, wisdom, and delight.

—Lisa Coffman

I met Bob Cumming at the Tennessee Mountain Writers Conference in 2017. We chatted, and he gave me his card, then ran out to his car to get me some books he thought I'd like. Bob is generous, kind-hearted, and intelligent—qualities that were obvious from that first conversation. His friendship became a blessing and a joy. When Iris Press published my book, *Available Light*, in 2019, Bob sent me some of his writing. It was then I realized his brilliance as a writer. I'm so happy this chapbook is being published, as now Bob's words have a permanent place to shine, and what he has long given to other writers comes back, full circle, to him.

—Sandy Coomer

What a pleasure to have a collection of the poems of Bob Cumming, a man whose generous belief in our poetry has always meant so much to us, his fellow writers. He and his son Beto kept our poetry in beautiful, carefully edited Iris Press books. Now we can keep Bob's words, hear his voice, and cherish them with the same attention.

—Susan Donnelly

As poet, essayist, scientist, engineer, teacher, editor, publisher, literary influencer, and lover of nature, Bob Cumming certainly meets my requirements for Renaissance man. At Iris Press he and his son Beto have constructed one of the most impressive catalogs of writers and poets to be found anywhere. I first discovered Bob's writing in his excellent essay "The Fall," published in *Still: The Journal*. Through Bob's influence I have been introduced to the genius of the underappreciated writers George Scarbrough, Joseph Enzweiler, and James Still.

—Mac Gay

I was privileged to call Bob a friend long before he also became a publisher. When Bob retired from a successful career at Oak Ridge National Lab and turned his brilliant and inquisitive mind to poetry, he, along with the help of his talented son, Beto, began to produce some of the most beautiful books of poetry available. An Iris Press book pleases in content as well as appearance. It will be a joy to have a volume of Bob's own words take its place among the excellent books he has brought into being. I am grateful to call Bob friend, editor, and publisher.

—Connie Jordan Green

I have not had the good fortune to meet Robert Cumming (Bob) in person, but I will not forget getting my first, thoughtful email from him after I queried him regarding my book, *Body Braille*, that he eventually published (along with the help of his gifted son, Beto). He was human, kind, sensitive. In a world where those qualities seem less and less the norm, and in the realm of publication where finances are sometimes paramount, I was quite struck—and impressed—by the personal and genuine exchange. In what I have read about Bob and through our subsequent correspondence, my admiration and respect for him as a publisher and person have only grown. I am truly grateful to call myself an Iris author—to have benefitted from Bob's (and Beto's) editorial acumen, kind stewardship, and fierce dedication to the literary arts.

—Beth Gylys

For decades, few people have been more passionate about and committed to the literary South (and, well, just literature!) as Bob Cumming. I am grateful and proud to be a part of the Iris Press family.

—Karen Head

Bob Cumming has been an inspiration, a superb mentor, and a good friend for over eighteen years. Much of what I understand and appreciate about poetry is because of him. I'm forever grateful.

—Cathy Ann Kodra

Bob Cumming was a faithful, integral member of the Knoxville-area writing community long before he undertook the roles of publisher and editor for Iris Press, bringing his scholarly mind of inquiry, study, and wisdom to readings, groups, and conferences. The presence of those you admire in such settings provides the spine and heart of a community, as Bob has done for me for over thirty years. I first heard the word "ekphrastic" from him, and its explanation, and he shaped my understanding and embrace of various forms, especially as a master of the sonnet! That he and his son, Beto, went on to shape the southern Appalachian literary landscape with the extensive Iris Press catalog is unquestioned, and he single-handedly rescued the treasured work of poet George Scarbrough from obscurity by reprinting his collections. I join the scores of other Iris authors in my deep appreciation for Bob's passion and expert eye.

—Linda Parsons

Bob Cumming has devoted the last quarter of his remarkable life to the noble goal of publishing the best literature he can find. His ambitions are of the purest sort: to serve the reading and writing community and to produce books that matter. The world is a richer place because of Iris Press and Bob Cumming's fierce devotion to it. We are all grateful to now see his own writing become part of that legacy.

—Rita Sims Quillen

—Robert B. Cumming, Jr.

Robert B. Cumming is a writer, editor, and publisher who resides in Oak Ridge, Tennessee. He is owner and publisher of the Iris Publishing Group, Inc., a small literary publishing company. He formerly was a research scientist at the Oak Ridge National Laboratory, where he served in several positions for thirty years. He holds two degrees in biology, with minors in geology and mathematics from the University of Florida in Gainesville. He has a PhD (1964) in cytogenetics and cell biology from the University of Texas in Austin, where he pursued post-doctoral work on chromosomal fine-structure and cell culture. He remains involved in science, particularly in genetics, ecology and evolution.

Cumming's writing in recent years has focused on poetry and essays. He is active in several regional and national writers' organizations and has been a workshop leader at various writing workshops. He has published poems and essays in many online and print journals. In 1981 he was founding president of the Society for Risk Analysis, a major scientific society, and editor-in-chief of its publication, *Risk Analysis*, an international, interdisciplinary scientific journal still published in New York.

He has worked at "day jobs" as a teacher (high school through post-graduate university), engineer, field biologist, molecular geneticist, risk analyst, and editor, among others. He has lived in the Appalachian South since 1964.

www.ingramcontent.com/pod-product-compliance
Lightning Source LLC
LaVergne TN
LVHW041311080426
835510LV00009B/957